Studies Inside the Consent of a Distance

Studies Inside the Consent of a Distance

Poems by

Ken Meisel

© 2022 Ken Meisel. All rights reserved.
This material may not be reproduced in any form, published,
reprinted, recorded, performed, broadcast,
rewritten or redistributed without
the explicit permission of Ken Meisel.
All such actions are strictly prohibited by law.

Cover design by Shay Culligan
Cover photograph by Anita Scott Meisel
Author Photograph by Anita Scott Meisel

ISBN: 978-1-63980-080-3

Kelsay Books
502 South 1040 East, A-119
American Fork, Utah 84003
Kelsaybooks.com

For Joy Gaines-Friedler, my favorite strange loop witness

Acknowledgments

Concho River Review: "James Brown, Performing at the Apollo, 1962," "That Perfume You Smelled in Grasse," "Maps"

Eunoia Review: "At the Water's Edge"

FutureCycle Press: The Malala Anthology: "Malala (Grief Stricken)"

Lake Effect: "Some Preliminary Notes on Wishing & Consent"

Muddy River Poetry Journal: "American Carnival," "The River Variation # 1," "The Water's Variation w/ Bird Feathers in it # 2"

Peninsula Poets: "Alive"

Poetry Society of Michigan: Five Year Anthology: "All the World, a Stage"

Poetry Society of Michigan News Letter: "Springtime Invocation: White Baneberry"

San Pedro River Review: "Bar Singer," "Two Portraits of Hunger," "The Angel of the Wonderful," "Fatherhood"

Soundings East: "The Light at the Edge of the Dining Room Table"

St. Katherine Review: "Valentine w/a Sentence in it," "Wilderness State Park Epistle"

Stoneboat Literary Journal: "January 20th 2017"

The Orchards Poetry Journal: "Witness," "Mayberry State Park Pastoral"

The Wayfarer: "Animals, Life, God, Etcetera"

Third Wednesday: "Studies Inside the Consent of a Distance"

"Witness" was nominated for a Pushcart Prize by *The Orchards Poetry Journal.*

When have you known the sweetness
of tapped maple or looked in the silent river,
saw what's hidden in the current?
—Joy Gaines-Friedler, "Teaching Young Adults at Risk,"
from *Capture Theory*

If you seriously believe, as I do and have been asserting for most of this book, that concepts are active in the brain, and if furthermore you seriously believe that people, no less than objects, are represented by symbols in the brain...and lastly you seriously believe that a self is also a concept, just an even more complicated one, then it is a necessary and unavoidable consequence of this set of beliefs that your brain is inhabited to varying extents by other I's, other souls...
—Douglas Hofstadter, from *I Am a Strange Loop*

Contents

Consent

Lust	15
Witness	17
Animals, Life, God, Earth, Etcetera	19
Studies Inside the Consent of a Distance	21
The River Variation # 1	23
Sequence: Five Tutorials from That Other World	26
Some Preliminary Notes on Wishing & Consent	39
At the Water's Edge	43
Mayberry State Park Pastoral	49
Fatherhood	54

Strange Loops

January 20th 2017	57
American Carnival	62
Two Portraits of Hunger, South Carolina	64
Malala (Grief Stricken)	68
Maps	69
The Grotesque	71
Bar Singer	74
I Am a Strange Loop	76
The Water's Variation w/ Bird Feathers in it # 2	82
Quartet for the End of Time	85

Alive

Alive	93
Springtime Invocation: White Baneberry	95
The Mural Painter Graffiti Artist	97
James Brown, Performing at the Apollo, 1962	100
The Angel of the Wonderful	103
What I Love About the Evening's Sunset (A Postcard)	106
That Perfume Fragrance You Smelled in Grasse	108
Valentine w/ A Sentence in it	112
The Light at the Edge of the Dining Room Table	115
Wilderness State Park Epistle	117
All the World, A Stage	120

Consent

Lust

In the thicket: small sweet birds
singing their chorus of secrets,

and the sun's dappled sheen—
crawling like lemon spumoni

across the leaves' shorn edges.
Mottled red shadows sprawling

over the collapsed fruit tree logs
and the fragrant piles of fruits

felled there, in the light's sugar.
All this coloration, spread out,

a plethora of aromas for taste.
Do you think the fallen angels,

dirtied by the soil upon landing,
felt with gilded wings their brand

new skin? Touched each other,
with finger tips seized by heat?

Collapsed, still later, and so exhausted
by this new-found enticement

with each other's sensual beauty—
by this stunning re-possession

of sensation warming their chilled
and ghosted finger tips with heat—

they slept in each other's wings.
And as dawn touched their new

bodies ever so slightly, waking
them and stirring them into this

first urge, the two hungry angels,
given over to it, acted upon it:

both of them sinned it awake.

Witness

I don't think I ever considered that the birds
were staring right back at me.

Everything has its eyes. Even the blind rock,
sitting so silently on the wooded path.

Even the fallen leaves, trying to remember; even
the eyeless dead fish, rotting blind in the pond.

All things gather, one at a time, to witness.
Even the parade of stars rising over a barn.

I don't remember what it was the woods said to me
when they warned me I'd been found there, alone,

trying to stop myself from telling the truth
of what I saw in myself. That I was just a lie.

But at the edge of the river, we witnessed it.
That I was afraid of accepting myself.

Everyone is afraid of accepting themselves
because they can't let themselves witness

just what they are, the woods said. And all I could do
was try to understand what couldn't be said.

Somewhere, out in the forest dark, we heard
coyotes screaming every laugh they had.

To witness, I think, is to follow a path
of allowance; whatever happens, just does.

It's so difficult to let a river canoe you.
But that's always what happens, isn't it?

Love's just what the breezes do, through trees,
by spreading rumors at the edge of the forest

that awakens awe inside empty space. I never knew it,
that love was primarily a movement experience.

Endings too, are witness experiences. I was told this
in Atlanta once, by a woman I was dating.

She made me fresh coffee and bid me goodbye.
Whispered to me the high clouds and sunshine

rise and dim slowly, *effortlessly,* like death.
Every river's flux, explains all that to me.

Animals, Life, God, Earth, Etcetera

You were lost in the woods, in biology class.
You don't even remember it, but the professor

told you you'd never find yourself
if you didn't make friends with earth's inhabitants.

I think two kids waltzed off, into the woods.
Down where the lanky river fidgeted

its nauseous ooze-body over fallen oak logs.
I think they were smoking fresh dope, and they

were high, and so whatever was to be cared
about, evaporated into that stinky smoke.

The river, nearby, enlarged itself over stone piles,
and a few ducks practiced floating on nothing.

You knelt down to witness a dirt-feast.
A handful of ants consuming a nearly dead bird.

The sun shifted position; leaves lit in flame.
A dead salamander: two birds pecking at it.

And the reluctant darkness inside the cold trees
whispered anything goes here; even death.

You couldn't see it then; you were too young;
but today you understand the earth's promise:

that it will confuse and mystify you until you
investigate it properly; until every part of you

becomes lost in its movements, its variations,
its attempts to make cycles out of what confronts

and even wrongs it. Even the birds in the trees
celebrated a dead squirrel's skull having been found.

The good true business of God is what Spirit does
with anything we think we can name and label.

Spirit lives in anything named, the dead squirrel
said to me when I moved its skull with a stick.

To name anything, is to get into a relationship
with all the *etcetera* living inside and about it,

said the wind in the trees; and the rattling leaves
answered that life and death dwell in them, like ghosts.

Mystery is the business of spirit, the dead skull
whispered to me. And even that's unnamable.

And the maggots in the squirrel skull bubbled out,
showing us that the beautiful and the ugly abide.

This confounding birth-beginning: it resources us.
This walk of one precious life on earth: it seeds us.

The solemn surrender to it—this dependable earth—
is what God is made of, the ash tree whispered.

We reach into Spirit's design, only by how we
live in the present; this hop, skip, jump into nature;

this emergent alignment, in a consent agreement
with the world, and all the wisdom it provides to us.

And every part of you is created—over and over—
by what you and your big heart do with all that.

Studies Inside the Consent of a Distance

I don't think I ever asked a tree permission to touch it.
Suddenly this is hurtful to me.
That I could fail a tree so,
like never noticing its bark ridges
as something of its personal skin, or its face,
and my fingers simply caressing it,
free from any deeper contemplation of it—
like studies inside the consent of a distance—
without ever even asking for consent.

Or the water's soft rumpling, just laying
so languidly there in its sleep-time morning bed;
I never asked it whether I could even climb into it,
to swim there in it, *within it;*
me somehow—just giving the vodka of my body
over to a lake's smooth likeness
in a kind of drunken assumption;
me, jumping into this strange water,
without ever even asking it.

Wishing is a kind of trickery; it
stirs a naked impulse in us.
Even the bird up there above me
eyes me warily, like I'd assume
power over its wings, its soul.

I'm thinking I'm sorry about this:
that a bird could mistrust me,
see in me that evil wish, that deed
to take, without consent, its order.

Living one's life by the shade of true love
is just a study inside the consent of a distance.
That we may exist together…is to *inhabit;* to *adore*.
To ask a blessing of the beautiful at stake here…
The world, so full of grantings: its faces, its lives.
That's all I'm saying, right here, right now.

All the trees, the birds, the waters, savor it.

To love is to consent to the distance of another.
And then, by slow degree, come safe closer.
This is my promise to the water, to the trees,
to the singing birds and to you.

The River Variation # 1

Thorough and immanent,
translucent and misted,

the river follows its lulling.
So full of transport pearls,

tossed pennies, glass bubbles,
and pieces of scatter and tithing

complete with mirrors
and indentations, it flows

and follows concourse; it
picks up bleedings and stitches,

shorn pieces of fabric, lost
earrings and gold tints;

it captures love letters and old
microscopic finger nails;

all the remaining after-shot
of a man's unrecognized

shirt, and the body of one
whose secret, kept inside skin,

no longer holds any verbal
council; floats aimless, away—

just a corpse drifting careless,
and relaxed as any other thing;

and the river bubbles and flirts
like a feral shaped she-tramp,

a tricky girl; and it changes
consent and consequence

in one tidal wave and swirl
against limit, wave over wave

into embayment and emptied zone—
like a nomadic History, a *Koan*.

And it seeks as it widens; it
ripples as it quiets; and it

wanders—an angel, a dervish—
in a whirlpool of wit and wind,

and it changes shape again to begin:
now it's a June bride mascara-lined

by willow hair and feather curls
made of lather and foam;

with horse legs kicked wide, inside
tree limes and skeleton bones

and arms—amorphous, ill-fitting—
in a wedding gown overthrown

and twig-sown; and with a character
re-arranging itself at whim:

now it's romantic and directed,
flirting and hugging with moss-

covered stones; with some old
deer's misshapen jawbone; and it

makes whole curlicues against
a cement water wall; it joins

the hard edge of the brick, and it
creates a baby of algae and grit;

and it flood-hugs a dam wall—
(a partner to raise a baby pile with;)

the father made of rock sludge
and sediment rock bits. And

the river—a wet comet's tail
splashed to flame by night stars

and by a moon wearing a mask
stretched across it like God—

holds Life and Death in it,
all Life and Light in it too;

and it's like a bejeweled
Queen Mother, scrawled

with gifts both great and small
in its uplift and sprawl:

and it's a lot like a Father's
good-intended long haul:

it carries a grand spark
of us all.

Sequence: Five Tutorials from That Other World

1. Fish

Floating signature of fins & silver shellacked scales—

some golden blue, some turquoise green,
some marbled pink, some wood alcohol brown

& some of your scales opaque as the rain
falling inside the sad stillness of water museums

that pass through your bewildered mouth
& in & through your fanning gills

forever pushing out the rich bubbled oxygen
that's dissolved in them

– like the gurgled splurge of the lake's spirit—

I see you as you winnow, like a silent apparition, beyond me.

& your operculum, like a rice paper sheet of glaze, covers your horrified

face as you go on shivering in the derelict moss light of this inland lake
where I watch you avoiding me.

Your nostrils are flaring open in a kind of derision;
in a style of contempt & escape, just like us;

& your spiny dorsal fin, resting atop your muscled body,

slices an invisible cross-divide between the light & dark
floating inside the low relief of the water's lavender & brown surface,

and your tail fin—an after-thought
swishing all your recent history away—

ejects all the rest of the loose swoosh of water & oxygen behind it

& also, the white mahogany of anus waste behind it
so that, when I look down at you,

all I can see is the fuzzy camouflage you create;
you see, it's like you *erase* yourself;

& your dorsal fins used for balance—fin rays
both spiny soft,

& branched like pieces
of sliced vegetable cut loose to swim—

cross-hatch & divide the world into a zinc-silver twilight
& an after-slough of waste-water & ganoid scales—

leaving, in the swirled mayhem of the water's curves behind you,
a confluence of polished bubbles & fizzed aftermath;

it's as if you ghost yourself as an act of forgetting;

& your two-chambered heart goes on pulsing the blood through it
while pumping the rest of the blood out of it

like the flung fist of a spirit dissolving;

& it beats so manic & rapid as you flatten, as you widen up
& you shoot under a fallen arcade of logs away from me;

& your teeth—for grasping, for tearing, for grinding
& for chomping every other gesture of fish or bubble

floating foolishly & aimlessly through them

never to return to life again   bite on;

& the thin prayer of you goes forward—silently, endlessly, soundlessly—
under the deep rasp ridges

& through the under water
interstellar transoms

& in & out of the shaded, pond grass cathedrals

that—just like in our world—

hold all the drowned submerged stars in them

& that,

just like ourselves, swimming vastly under those cathedral stars, we pray to, we make love to,

& that, like you, we think of, as God.

2. Bird

Developed from the scaly covering
    of lizards
        you clamored up to rise like a sunburst
            to the soaring light

    just like we are trying to do right now
        years upon years behind you;

and your flight feathers, strung and hung from oil-stone arrows
    and a barbed mesh
        woven tightly to form a firm structure

    of contour feathers—
        red, blue, yellow, orchid, emerald green and otter's pink—

must have bewildered
        your stone-dumb lizard relatives

    still stuck in the cribbed muck and emulsified swamp droop

of the tropic's humidified forest.
    And your body, taking off from a bloated tree stump,
        must have resembled a rising

    ecstatic yellow comet;—
        your air sacs, thin as *craquelure tiles*

and your hollow bones—strait, radial, spiraled
    and corkscrewed
        like tiny incised wires

    inside your body's lean aeronautic tabernacle—

sent you soaring outward,
    just like a soul on fire,
        far, far away from yourself.

And like a fire-flamed meteor

suddenly hurled above a tree canopy
or down a gulch of starved stumps

or way across a rolling parfait of lichen rock
and grassland green,
you must have resembled

what God saw when his angels,
condemned, flew free.

And just like the water's very rapid stream,
or like a leaping water spout at the stretch mark
of burst and billow,

you must have spiraled up—a radiant crease in spectacular flight—
your body feathers

corked with after-shafts both lithe and lean
as the wind's ecstatic emotion;

and your feather-rump,
caked with mud and weed
and a stalk-grass
capable of a sudden wiggling and a shaking
—just like us—

must have jiggled all the dirt from it in a swift cleansing;

and your wicked tail and a coronation crown cut in royal pomposity
above two claws curled tight below tucked wings—
fixing you to your body's taut sculpture—

must have steadied you as you perched stealthily
on an evergreen out crop,
readying yourself for flight.

And your smooth belly, pumped up into a prideful breast,

and those greedy feverish eyes capable of seeing everything you wanted or despised
        —just like us—
must have fixed their gaze on the inexplicable
        —just like us—
so as to see the glory at the other end of some mystery;

        and you must have transfigured—in a practiced flight—
    and went soaring over a convergence fire
        as you arranged yourself
            to explode in blaze and flame

against the bleak unfazed horizon
    where the sun had set, a walnut yellow.

Every quality about you
    so capable of transfiguring—
        just like one of God's fevered, melodious angels
            born down here to roam the branches,
                the soft woodland glades,
                    the solitary rivers.

    It makes me write about you; you're a marvel to me.

    And now when you lift right up,
        alert with vainglorious and grandiose ambition
like a sudden bullet flight of light,
        your sudden wing pattern breaking apart
    in an aeronautics line
        of bronze-gloom tracing
      and untamed rapture,

        I must confess to you
that you *do* disappear in a noiseless operatic splendor.

And you resemble *us* when we arc and dive
        into the pond's engorged reflection—

      vanishing too, into oblivion's core
          like we always seem to do when we are trying to
    die—
          only to be reborn again, alive.

And when you soar *upward*,
    just like we do
        when we fly in our airplanes—
copied no doubt
        from the silver sachet fragrance
            of what you truly are—

the both of us fly aimless
right into the sky's vast uncharted infinity

      like sudden, resplendent
          exuberant angels taking flight,
              right into this divine

      unexplored light upon endless light.

3. Cicada

Small emperor of tall tree tops,
you sizzle when you sing

for the day's last excited declining;
it's like your olive green body

has been lit on sacrificial fire,
and your one torched musical note

has been torn from you by a
kind of day-long body torture.

Is it devotion that arises in you?
Or is it the insistent, brutal torment

of the winged assassins that fly
so close to you and gouge you with their

hungry pointed beaks, their talons
made of cruel wax cartilage?

Is it God that breaks your body's
figure down and tears your throat apart

with all this wired buzzing racket?
Or is it some other insect goddess

that you've hopelessly fallen in love with
inside your intense globe eyes

and your wings of spit and crystal?
Is this what makes you sing?

Once, one of you fell on me;
you fell like a defeated astronaut.

And when you landed,
you were so dead and dry

I thought I'd caress you
in a warm bath of milk and honey,

just to awaken the life in you.
Once I found another of you

alive and paralyzed on the
pavement; you were writhing

in agony, just like a fallen angel
unable to inhale this humid air—

you injured body so still-born
by radiance and by electric singing

to God—and, as I lifted you up,
you started again with this ceaseless

buzzing; it was like you were
sizzling a sutra to the falling

sunlight of the day's last color.
It was as if all the life in you

would cease and rev itself
– again, again—

to whatever opened prayer
could grab and hold it

in exalted awe and terror,
in silenced solitude, in death.

4. Cat

I move lithe and delicate
   through the soft wet grasses
of the early May morning,
   my stark eyes lasered
on the robin that's drinking
   from the fountain,
while the soft, white cherry
   blossoms fall—so simply—
into the water below.
   In the lemon glow distance
the steeple bells of the Catholic
   church bramble on,
announcing the hour.
   Still farther, as I slink past
the lower edges of the deck,
   my olive-tinted eyes
fixed like steel on this bird,
   I can hear the Moslem
calls to prayer,
   and the leveled shriek
of a police siren
   ribboning through the stillness
of the morning,
   as if coloring the gentle world
with a selfish screaming.
   Above me, I hear the lovers
in their lavender sheets
   returning again to their
love-making ritual,
   and I hear the last interrupted
ricochet of crickets
   chirruping beneath
the pink mauve of the peony
   that's blossoming here
like an outstretched pieta,
   and, a pigment of ants,

greedily mouthing the sugar
   of the praying flowers
into their salted mouths
   like rancid little piranhas,
and I see, with a quick glance
   of my alert green eyes,
a whole pigment of ants
   consuming all that grips
the flowers taut
   in a tight fist of hearts
seemingly unafraid to awaken,
   as if the peony, itself,
could birth the new savior
   into this sullen, injured world,
or hold the tumult
   of something dumbstruck
unto death in its somber,
   green-stroke of leafy arms.
The rabbit-toned skin of dawn
   opens quickly, with this glorious
sunlight rising inside it,
   as if offering one more hour
to this world of green grass and trees
   and fountains with birds
sipping to quench their thirst.
   Nobody in the world
can comprehend
   the luminous glow
flickering through my pupils,
   nor the hunger,
set like lettering quills
   in my rows of white teeth
as I leap and grab it,
   this robin,
in my coal black mouth.

5. Gray Squirrel & Red Hawk

I watched her from my window as she scooted down
a maple tree, & zoomed across the autumn ground

like a curious little meteor. Her fur coat, the color of soot-ash,
& her bushy tail, gray, with silver-tipped hairs.

     She was nosing
under a pine tree for nuts, for gnawed acorns or tulip tree seeds,
& I loved her like a little sister as she buried each nut & tamped, for & back,
a bed for them so that she could sniff them out when the winter
snows came & buried them &, up above, in the ramshackle

nest that she'd weaved from twig scraps & other wasted wood-
clutter left strewn under the tulip trees & the lofted maples,
I could watch as the bigger boy squirrel—her favored suitor—
came rushing downside to chase her like a hurricane
around the lazy park as the October sun, hesitant, deliberate,
flirted up & down the slopes of the wayward park grass
where the monkey bars & the lazy swing set—farther out—
was a metal city. & she was young & fresh & just a girl come out
from the abandoned woodpecker den she'd grown so very
beautiful in, & she was peppered & sprightly, & so faithfully
playful that all the boys wanted her. & so they'd chase her
through the wild canopies of the leafless maples & up & over & across
& deep into the romantic pine tree bedspread of silk needles
& then down, across the muddied dirt &, I'd see her,

     so excitable—
& her little foot prints stretched on the ground when bounding,
& her paired back feet paw-printed just ahead
of her twinned foreprints; & she'd race ahead of the boys,
just, I think, to play, for she was so joyous & so alive,
& on the last day, from my window, I watched gently as she
shivered & she sniffed & she dug for something,

& the hawk there, sitting still as a feathered crossbow,
        dropped
& it landed straight on top of her &, with its pointed arrow,
it pierced her left eye & the eye glazed over, into that odd,
blind, gelatinous haze that the after-life must be made of

        &
I don't know why, because the hawk just sat there, then—
thoughtless, & already forgetting what it'd just done,
       & then it lifted up
like an emperor already indifferent to the afternoon's

bored patina & it flew absently, easily away, over the swing set,
       & she just lay there,
her bushy squirrel's tail like a girl's woolen scarf wrapped
      soft around her nose,
       to shake a bit, & die.

Some Preliminary Notes on Wishing & Consent

> "The political institutions of any nation are always menaced and are ultimately controlled by the spiritual state of that nation"
> —James Baldwin

1.

Because a wish is just the experience of *deserving,* expressing itself,
all the ducks, squatting here on the embankment,
fly and scatter away when I step closer to them.
It's as if my wish and their wishes collide, and there
is friction, a scattering apart of the union,
which reminds me, always, of what love does
when one person, faltering at the edge of his wishes,
transgresses against another, and there is a fight…

Every fight is a wish, uncoupling itself into expression.
Or opposition, oppression, synthesis, polarization, *action.*

It's as if *wish,* which must be the feminine undercurrent
of springtime, and it must hold the masculine, too,
and the sunlight, the action, the reaction, and all the rest
of what follows it, knows no real morality; it's just *impetus*…

Every wish is the expression of creation, and, so, *God,*
which is just the wish formation of the Universe, the
name it gives itself out of utter namelessness, wishes upon us
one or two great days in our life where what we wish for,
because it's part of the great stream of universal livingness,
comes back to us as the cup and saucer of *knowing it.*

That's why the woman at the strip club, the dancer,
sparkling herself into one of the forms of Master and Slave,
which is like a board game God must have invented
in order to study just what types of forms wishes
will take and command when tossed against each other,
urges me to come inside by sucking on her middle
finger, which makes me suddenly think of a lollipop…

Every wish I can think of deserves itself into expression,
even my wish to touch the green back of a duck,
or the soft lips of a stripper…it's just the impetus, seeking life,
and even the wish of the cat and what *he* wants,
hiding back there in the honeysuckle, watching all this.
And when I think of God, what comes to mind is
one or two great days where I *knew* what my wish was,
and I acted on it, to get it, and something was made, *better*.

*

When one person wishes himself into something,
another person, maybe his wife, ceases in her becoming,
and then there is friction, collapsing, repulsion.

That is just one of the laws of inauthenticity. At least
that's what Heidegger said, once, in a big book,
in fact, the book I'm watching this co-ed read at Starbucks.

Every marriage dances this one little wish out, and some get
their innocence back, that is, the promise of their authenticity,
and some disappear into a fog of self-perpetuated invisibility.
It's because the essence of authenticity always involves intimacy
and not invisibility—although it is only through invisibility,
that is, the falling away from the self, that authenticity floods back.

And God, because of restlessness and curiosity, adds and divides
in order to understand that intercourse, the act of making
wishes come into being, always moves in an infinity loop…

That's just the way creation *looks,* whether it's good or bad.

2.

Consequences are just human wishes made just and fallible…

And every crime you or I commit will be *some* violation of consent,
and that's because consent means *together-feel*. No act, no wish,
can harm, if two come together to feel their mutual strength and truth,
and whatever goodness into light that all-together-feeling brings.

And all crime is a violation of one, or more than one law of the Universe.

And perhaps we can barely help it, so impulsive we are to feel
what it must feel like to explode like a balloon, bursting with stars.

Or to set to fire whatever beauty parlor we can't contend with.

And that's because consent demands restraint first, and then risk.
And every wish is what is answered by a consent to provide.

Wisdom, I think, is what the hands do, when praying a wish.
And generosity is what the heart exults, within the wish alive.

*

Nothing should ever be done that tears apart the fabric of innocence,
is what every crime I ever studied, exhorted back to me.

I wouldn't lie about this in any mirror at any truck stop, or in any
Beauty salon with my Irish face staring back at me, trying anyway
to betray me. Consent is what the hands do, when covered over
with the blood of a thousand hurts preceding any new wish.

Consent, wrapped in a love-wish, offers a loyalty to innocence.

And that is why this stripper, talking to me, and also these ducks,
here, in this poem, are just symbols for what is innocent,
and also for what is destructible, in just one instant action.

Nothing in creation—creation being just the wish of what's
transformable, transforming—escapes the cold hard scrutiny
of those who witness it. It's always best to remember this,
and that's because every wish coming to life requires an audience.
And every audience is but a spectator to a People's History.

That's why, by the way, on the game board of Master and Slave,
the man and the woman dance awake, into whatever form
they wish to be. And so does America, so does Christopher
Columbus, in fact, representing the Western World, or Spain,
when he beats a dark skinned boy in the shallow surf
of a tropical West Indies island, way back in October, 1492,
and then he writes of it in his journal in order to show
every one of the natives looking on, that is, the young topless
girls and their old grizzled fathers adorned in their necklaces
and beads, just what the wish of subjugation and dominion
will look like, i.e., how it will take shape, and be formalized and locked
into *perpetuity,* you know, in the sacred name of the Queen.

Every wish, therefore, is in the name of the King or Queen.
And therefore, there's no escaping that wishes are always
born by Directive. And they're always, you know, in the name
of a God—perhaps the King and Queen *inside* a God—

maybe the God inside any man or woman, expressing it—
whatever God that *is*, you know, whoever is becoming it.

Whatever that union holds—you know—as sacred, in the immediate.

*Sacred, meaning, whatever is set apart for the service
and / or the worship of a deity and made and / or declared as holy.*

And what ever is born of *that,* carries a model of consent.

At the Water's Edge

The water's a chilled,
        metallic shale today—
                a moody luster,

it's greasy, flexible—
        with small, irritated fragments
                of finely-grained granite

floating in it: red, silver,
        even sparkles of purple, olivine,
                as it catches the strident

gleaming of sunlight radiating down
        from a thickening strata
                of storm clouds

that are moving across the surplus
        of open water;
                and, what's more:

the water's black
        tourmaline waves,
                leaping over one another

and crashing up against the bullied
        moorings,
                have floating ducks

in them—
        just simple pintails
                moving upward

and downward
        into the water's heavy
                rock shatter—

and every now and then—
        when I stray left
                and right with my hands

holding tightly
        to the railing
                like I'm line-dancing

on the railing of a cruise ship
        to the locomotion
                of the sundry waves—

one duck emerges again, head doused
        with the igneous grease
                of the sub-surface

wave-lather of the water's
        lopsided, carnival drop
                and glow,

and, when I see this, I think
        we too must be like this,
                ducking ourselves

inside the murmur of the water's
        fluorite copper
                and its cathedral depth

and deep into its zinc oxide of uncertainties,
        and we must need to dive in again:
                to even deeper

turbulent substrata—
        especially when we forget
                that our personalities

are made of rocks and stones
        capable of great
                stubborn withholding

and an even greater
        smash-mouth crash
                and re-emergence;

and isn't *that* what we're so bewildered
        about, time in and out again
                as we ponder

how we change—
        because, inside us,
                our inner thoughts

are really just flying fish
        with lumachelle wings,
                with flames-of-wandering,

and every thought in us
        longs, one day, to become
                totally undressed and undone—

just like waves fracturing, bit by bit,
        under the aquamarine
                tumult of a bang-a-gong.

And once, I almost drowned. It was
        when I was alone and swimming
                and being careless—

I'd roamed out too deep—and suddenly
        I was bottomless,
                no duck's webbed feet

beneath me, and I knotted up, out of fright,
        and I went under.
                And so I retreated

the way we always do when we
        are humiliated or frightened,
                our illusions, busted,

and we surrender. And it was only
        my incentive against anything *like* that—
                a drowning, a slipping under,

a vanishing—
        that rescued me,
                and I found my direction again,

I swam back to the shore.
        And shivering there, wrapped
                in a towel,

I could feel
        the hard truth
               that there are knots

we can tie around us, or become tied in
        out of a foolishness in us—
                like being in the deep

of something beyond our capacity—
        and they're fatal knots
                we can't untie or get out of

without another consent, another agreement,
        or an accord that frees us,
                and that's a world not any good,

it's a world of our foolishness
        that misaligns us with the power
                of emotion, or water.

But that was a long time ago,
        when I was at the water's edge
                of something too familiar in me

competing with
        something as yet to be known,
                and I found it, good enough.

And, at the water's edge then,
        deep in the finely-grained
                granite of myself,

I found it good enough—that I could
            actually drown too, in what I was,
                        or wasn't, all the same.

But this water, rough-housing
            itself against the pier,
                        here at the edge,

lumbers effortlessly
            through the quicksilver
                        shoulders of its own

inexorable trek across
            the horizon's greater shrilled
                        steel-and-glass,

just like it's attempting to know itself
            in closeness, in consent,
                        and in distance.

And I see the visual
            imagery of it all:
                        the wing-scatter

of sea gulls flying into gloam:
            hundreds of them,
                        rising up

and nose-dropping
            into beautiful waters
                        as hard as glass.

And I leave something of me,
            some foolishness of me
                        out there so it can rest,

and be found again by someone
            other than me who needs it.
                        And at the water's edge—

today—now fully safe again—
    I watch the water's
        purl and plume

hammering and plowing
    under the sea gulls resting
        atop it,

and I study the consent of just what
    it must take to float,
        like gulls,

above all this
    liquid happenstance,
        into who we are.

Mayberry State Park Pastoral

"For this was the beginning of the burning time"
—James Baldwin

One after another the teenage boys
        and the girls bound out

of their cars in cheerful pairs
        and they slip slide and slope

into the dark woodland forest
        holding each other's hands

so that they can snuggle down again
        on a dried out log

and they can slurp their bottles
        of cheap beer

and smoke their first cigarettes
        with one another

and practice holding up the lighter
        for each other to try.

All this begins when the yellow-throated
        warblers arrive again to sing

their wichity-wichity-songs at the edges
        of the forest where the fallen

tree branches have formed tangled bundles
        of refuse, and the lichen-drizzled

mounds and rodent dens hide small voles
        that watch the sky for hawks that prey

And one after another, the teenage boys
        and the girls lean very closely

into each other's warmed faces
        to practice kissing each other's

lips at first gently and wisely, and then,
        still later—after the summer

has baked these woods into a color
        of heat and shamrock green frenzy—

their kisses become wet and unruly
        as they move so close together

they can barely keep their deep breathing
        separated into a rhythm,

and one after another, like new England asters
        suddenly ablaze with red flowers

blooming up expansive stalks that grow
        wild to dominate the trail-side,

the girls and the boys become awesome
        in what they seem to carry.

Nobody seems to want to understand it—
        that these children *will it*—

this emergent urge for growing. But they
        continue on with it—this kissing

that is a practicing for what their
        younger lips will to become as adults:

these lips made from an under-structure of cellular layers
        and a stratified squamous epithelium,

and a cupid's bow, where the sensual upper lip
        rises triumphant and erotic

over the rugged lower lip where both meet the face
    at the reddish vermillion border

and something—like a narrow crack—wiggles up
    into a galvanized smile that laughs;

and these lips will one day become angel fish
    swim-kissing to another—a partner—

and so the boys and the girls, under the deep shade
    of these woods, keep up their

escapades of kissing in hiding spots
    where unseen mealworm beetles

freeze and stir under the rotting log bark,
    and mantidflies slink and slide

across the rotting forest floor
    and grab other insects

into their vices to eat;—
    and, beyond this, where the new moon

rises like a snow trillium over the loud swamp
    and the last birds fly down

through the Rayleigh scattering
    to merge, like sharp lightening bolts

with the reddish seduction of twilight
    and with the physical sensation

of a nightfall becoming lunar,
    you can *hear* their voices—these kids

who are practicing what it is to make their lips
    become the wandering angel fish

that seek another person
        for the pair-bonding of a night

that will, one day, take them
        all the way to love's borderland

of heaven;—and you can hear their shyness
        and their innocence, too,

and that quick laughter
        that bows as it dances

into flirtatious display,
        and also that miraculous elixir

inside their love songs composed
        of hoot owls and moon beams,

giving to each of them all these soft melodies
        they hum after dark—

(this is something none of us sitting safe in our chairs
        should ever forget:

it's what mystifies us against them
        forgetting who *we* once were . . .)

and it's that unstoppable power that ignites
        in their eyes and vapors us—

yes, this is something none of us should
        ever omit or forget

because it was once that very same torch
        in our life, and in *our* bodies too,

and, so, we shouldn't be cynical of it,
      nor mistrust it in fear—

and that it baptizes them—each and every one
      of their little fires—into life.

Fatherhood

The abyss found me. I'd been thirsting for it for days,
without even knowing it. It sought me after midnight

in smoky after-hours jazz clubs, in cold pick-up bars,
and through the soft, expressed touch of lips.

Maybe it was attempting to show me that one must give in
to the consent, and to the expressed abyss of another.

What it requires of someone: that they must *give*—
if they're to be guided by the greater impulse of the abyss.

I can't recall moving from the indifferent to the engaged,
but that's what the leap into the abyss does;

it understands being alive is about the original abode of life,
that wellspring, that pleasing, shapeless glimpse

into the unknown, making itself expressively known in the self.
Didn't it tell me I was just an amorphous shape?

Something bendable to a likeness; a responsive miracle?
When she came crawling up to me at night, 3 am,

her hair in a mess, my daughter reported to me that there
was a witch in her room. It dogged her at the abyss.

Not tigers, not lions, not bears; just a bad witch.
We crawled back over the floor to get it, that witch.

Sprayed it with rose petal water, just to erase it.
Suffering, sadness, soul-searching; these are nothing

to a witch. We sprayed it dead, there in the abyss—
where the immense journey is; that kind of love.

Strange Loops

January 20th 2017

    Inauguration Day

The morning's light today is a whiskey hue,
        and the dirt—resembling pistachio
                and a mix of leaf lettuce—

seems to silence, become soft, and gentle,
        as if in tranquility.
                Last week, at a riotous rally,

I watched one group of people
        swearing at another group,
                as if the total voice of the protest

was widening, splintering, torquing—
        and responding to frequencies
                outside of its capacity to tolerate.

The total voice, so elastic, stretched now
        to extreme ends—
                as one man shouted out

at another his personal
        notion of what makes rightness
                a providence

of the *singular*. Is rightness always
        in the singular form? Does one's
                singularity determine

all notions of rightness? How is this so?
        The solitary bird, sitting
                on the fence

in my backyard, offers an expressive
        quality like no other
                before him.

What to make of this? Is he correct?
    His tune, the final
        say-so on the morning's

rally of music? Who'd dare arbitrate
    such a question as to which bird's
        short aria is right?

Which becomes the best one? My neighbor's car,
    so blue it competes
        with a nascent sky?

Who's right there? Must it be blue sky,
    or the total blue cobalt car—
        as the *best* order of correctness—

that triumphs over *all* variations of blue?
    My wife's eyes, too—so *azure*—
        better than the whole sea?

These fingers I have, soft, curious,
    so often trespassing
        when I least expect it—

trying to find where it is that *rightness*
    and *correctness* coincide,
        when I pet my little cat.

When people clash, the voice, like an alarm,
    explodes, it shatters.
        We have no consistency

to consider it, terrified as we are—
    when the world we thought we knew
        becomes *someone else's*.

Theft is the greatest fear we know.
    Not abandonment, not murder,
        theft: of our idea of correctness.

Once, on a beach, and stealing a rock,
        I felt an artificial grandiosity
                spark me.

Only then did I require acquisition.
        My inner voice of restraint, dulled,
                denying me

any other chance to even
        question what happens to me
                when this grandiosity—

this coldness of estrangement—
        curls my fingers around a rock
                or a stone to *take it*. Throw it.

Estrangement, grandiosity, theft,
        these conditions that compel us
                to—well—injure and steal.

When the protesters
        had had enough of shouting,
                they hurled things:

soda cans, rocks, old rubbish, expletives.
        Nothing seemed to settle them
                until a boy, a child—

perhaps six or seven—sat down
        in the middle of the littered avenue
                to sing and rock himself.

It wasn't really protest: it was another
        form of self-engagement
                he'd tranquilized himself in.

I watched him succeeding.
        Is it that we just *can't* calm down—
                until one expressive quality

envelopes the qualities of another one?
        The autonomic nervous system in us
                so fickle, so impressionable?

The rest of our mind—
        captured
                by hues of distress, love?

By a simple change of color tone or hue?
        Once I watched this be true
                when one of my cats

stopped wrestling with her older brother,
        and she started licking him:
                the small pink tongue,

a form of affective counterpoint, *a tone*—
        setting up the immersion stage
                into a gentler result.

When the protesters quit—mostly because
        the whole lot of them had lost
                the grip on a quality

of voice, toned in harangue, so *ignited*—
        I wandered over to the little boy
                still sitting there, rocking,

and I asked him what his name
        could be.
                In a diffuse threshold

made of hush and whisper,
        he pretended he was a parrot,
                imitating

what he felt beneath
        all the maelstrom voices,
                which was distress.

Nothing right or wrong
        in distress. Just images of violence
                followed by tender soothing.

He'd lost his mother
        In the melee. *I'll rock you*
                I said to him. *We're both lost.*

American Carnival

I am the transient mania
that comes to town in the springtime
when the trees offer to the gloomy world
their whorls of sap green leaves,
and the small orphaned plants,
rising from the wet, mottled soil,
split their fingerling leaves
through the dense wet mud like the tendrils
of angels, escaping their dungeons.
Some caprice of stillness insists me here.
Something of me protests the perishing world.
I set in space my picnic table of Ferris wheels
and merry-go-rounds and circus tents
in the parking lots of the churches,
while surrounding me, the lots of cars
with their catfish faces and their pike tailfins
sit still, like schools of two-toned fish.
I offer the world its strange heights.
I bring to the world the tilt-a-whirl
and the floral caricature of carousals and twists,
and bumper cars and giant spinning tea cups
where the unimagined world exists again.
Something of me comes from nightmare,
something from the snippets of dreams
forgotten, in the glare and glaze of waking.
The animals along the fence line
recognize me as the floating signatures
of the world's broken fragments—
coming back to life force again—
like grotesque pieces of the world's disarray.
Even the policemen, like blue bishops,
their billy sticks at hip, stand still,
and they allow the sky above them
to break open with the strange
bellowing glow of shrieks and lights.
Watch, if you can, the little girls
in their pink dresses,

gathering together like honeysuckle
to climb up onto the Ferris wheel
for their lift off to heaven.
Notice the way that their mothers
fidget their slender fingers
into their small, irritated purses
for cigarettes, and do observe
the style that they employ
as they hover intimately together
like lacquered white swans,
chattering in groups. Watch as the boys
in their fringe coats and their coonskin hats
nudge up close to the gun gallery,
rifles in hand, to shoot at the small
sanguine faces of the tin clowns
moving up and down like convicts
in a frozen, drunken laughter,
and notice the rows of stuffed animals
lined up like rewards on the shelf behind—
a strange lonesome zoo
waiting to be taken. Catch the Carney
with his missing front tooth hawking
out the tickets for the bang-a-gong.
Notice as the fathers, like hydraulic pipes,
strengthen themselves with fat cigars
and brown bottles of beer as they line up,
in muscled pairs, to take turns
with the gigantic silver hammer
to bang the bell as hard as their mighty
might can take them—so that the ball,
like a mercury sun, can rise up
again to smash the uppermost top
of something imperishable—
and listen to the world's echo chamber
like a conundrum, banging on,
as the ball, hitting the bell, rings.

Two Portraits of Hunger, South Carolina

On a lonesome stretch
of South Carolina

back country,
surrounded

by cotton,
yellow-eyed grass

and bees,
I see the girl

approaching me
down her

front porch
like she's a ghost

in white, threadbare
hand-me-downs.

She's carrying
a baby

in her skinny arms
like it's

a life-size
salamander.

She gazes at me
with lunatic eyes,

a sanitarium's
stare,

cracks open
a smile

like it's
a mud snake

winding all
around me.

What is hunger
if we refuse

to face it,
face-to-face?

We are bound
together in a ring

that neither binds us
nor frees itself,

and that is the
style of our hunger,

and it creates these
strange loops we live.

A boy circles
a lonesome party store

on a bicycle.
Does one-wheelers.

Spits his gum out.
Maybe he's ten—

his skin, black
as a hard-shelled

mud turtle,
eyes green

as a large mouth bass,
river birch arms

waving leaf-hands
at me,

like he's in the wind.
He lights up a smoke.

Calls out to me—
do I have any extra

dollar bills in my deep
pockets, to give?

Blows halos into the air,
like he's exhaling

every thought from his
hungry alligator brain.

Rides circles around
the chiseled road

where the party store
sits half-abandoned

like a stranded,
land-bound boat,

just like he's a pirate,
a bandit on the hardcore

wheel of life.
And the girl

with the salamander
baby in her arms

laughs at me
like she's insane—

someone the afternoon
eats,

like a hysterical
star.

Malala (Grief Stricken)

> On October 9th 2012, Malala Yousafzai
> was shot in the head and neck
> in an assassination attempt by the Taliban

"*Grief stricken* is a name I'd use for it,"
the cleric said to his student

as they strolled through the rose garden
to examine the stomped roses.

Above them, the empty blue sky,
around them, noisy school buses.

"Someone must have come here
under cover of cloak or domain,

perhaps enraged at the sight of roses
where before there was just rubble,

or perhaps it was just the old gardener
who could not tolerate—" that was

the word he used in conversation
with his student—"could not tolerate

the way the earth must always renew
itself in beauty," and kneeling down

the cleric held the rose head in his
hand to highlight the red twirls of it

to his student who kneeled there
beside him, eyes bright and curious,

and he called it *feminine,* by the pronoun,
Malala—"this condition of the world

we find ourselves involved in,
this one enduring rose that survived."

Maps

Take for instance the map of a woman
who is assaulted and raped on a bus

and tossed off into weeds to re-assemble
what has been seized and stolen from her

and how it might be that—at her passing—
that map might join the larger street map

of the universe of living beings attempting
to navigate the portals of consciousness

and self awareness. How might that map
evolve itself? Perhaps through trial and pain?

Perhaps through reactive confrontation
or policy formulation which promotes more

counter reactive mapping?…as if mapping
is really not *dissimilar* to the manner by which

crystals replicate themselves under turbulence
and heated pressure beneath the earthen brow

of geologic inner conflict?...or perhaps the
mapping we as human beings endure is created

in reactive empathy and horror—those larger
narratives of what we *are* to one another—or

perhaps through the chemical fits and starts
of consciousness which under the microscope

resemble dendritic spurts, lit up in spiked neon—
and eeking their way up through torrid neurological

heat—which is what our brains feel when we
confront what is primitive and unruly in us—

we feel heat—and what we *do* with that heat
becomes part of the larger map we all walk

together, no matter where we stand—whether
waiting in line at the bank to cash a check

or seated on a bus after watching a boy
confront the primitive rage of a Bengal tiger

in a movie called Life of Pi somewhere
far away—in India—far away and yet so close

to where I write the final line of this poem—
as I confront the mapping of my own heat.

The Grotesque

Do you remember what we saw there,
holding hands together

in the dreary, olive noontide?
That the sea, a sad effluvium

of plastic refuse, had turned itself
into a gray morass, de-composing

in the near twilight, and it had settled
silently like a sad fog to the shore?

How the lovers, embracing, co-authored
the fires up in the hills, and the protests,

everything, seemed at first to be
the enterprise of an uprising, a gate?

Even the shore, lit up in flaming candles,
appeared beautiful, a floral banquet.

And the concierge there—tuxedoed—
held open a paper gate that we entered,

and sat us at various, white table-clothed
tables with decanters of wine there.

And we listened to TVs—back behind us—
where the world's conversation

about art and society
had turned into a quarreling throng

of people drowning one another out
over subjects like culture and sex,

war and religion—like a routing out
of love's final, lost remaining

languor. The grotesque,
like a carnival, parades always—

and the major, with his armies,
marches outward against time.

Its ultimate prisoner, the imago—
all our vibrant, inner identities.

That the grotesque takes the body—
all the beauty of it—like a parasite.

Thievery, the biggest sin, being
the ultimate happy-hour party.

Even the protests took on a
brutish, occupational, angry tone.

Appropriation is the first resort
of the cloaked thief, the magpie.

And politics is the hostile aim
of the few, against the many.

And in the salons, even the birds
in their cages resorted to imitation.

Style, as ornamentation, turned
cheap, within a rancid, vulgar luster.

The mouth, as a body part, a hole,
became the focal point of all news.

And the original, like a rare pearl,
was muted, muddied in the sand.

And the Angels of Mercy—so shy—
withered back, into the laurel hills.

We were given royal treatment,
a dinner party, away from it all.

And that the dancers, spinning,
spun a seed from the cocoon.

Some kind of seed that would
unsettle us against each other.

Would make us join tribes: as
a kind of affiliation, in kind.

That's what we saw there, odd,
so dangerous, that the grotesque

masquerades as a belonging,
tempting us to all dine.

Bar Singer

To become as baroque as this singer,
strumming her guitar outside the bar

while the customers line up, shove in,
mark their seats for the main act—

a rock band from Muskego made
mostly of bar brawls and metal noise

and the fumbled rage behind all envy—
I'd have to undress the marked frets

of my body the whole way, so that I
would fall up the stairs—all of me—

just like she's going to do in an hour
as the patrons yell and throw darts.

Maybe we have to fall up the stairs of life,
just to move from the lower rungs of it.

And as she sings her way into the evening's
immaculate drunken approval,

she and I'll become uplifted into the hurt
but magnificent luminous bareness

of one note now, simple, yet extravagant.
Isn't that always the ordeal of the true

singer-song writer? To be ornamental,
even when the breaking heart's

wreckage, so undone, delivers itself
to midnight and a lonesome guitar solo?

She's a brunette, an introvert, psalmic,
an improbable opening act for this

all male bar band, especially as she
lifts her voice in a plaintive hum-singing—

just like a resplendent thrush—and she
winds her voice around the song's crisp

trail lines by twisting *affect* all around it.
She's deliberate, so evangelistic: as if each

word, each one noun, were a history,
a picturesque fume, a flame with no flag

except that lone flag of sweetness—all of it—
like a song I could climb into, forever.

I Am a Strange Loop

Look: the young lovers, strolling
        down the beach
                holding hands together

blend homogenous, and they lose
        colors, and their differences
                seemingly *blend*—

so that as I watch them, I lose
        track of where his color
                loses itself to hers.

Groups that emerge together,
        combine sectors,
                they proliferate

in sameness; and isn't that the aim
        of empathy's apparatus
                of capture?

To materialize something of the one—
        some individualized coloration—
                inside the color

display of the other's domain?
        This couple's co-existence
                forms a network.

She's losing her softer body
        with the larger inhabitation
                of his left shoulder

as they stop to embrace
        at the shore line
                where the waves—

dusty bronze—dome and crash
        against the edge
                of the beach

and re-arrange it in a study
        of clap and re-emergence
                into new colors

not quite yet fully formed—
        because the tumult of blending
                won't yet allow it.

Empathy's just like that:
        it's a knee-jerk blending—
                of one wave action

moving sideways into another wave.
        It's like a vigorous form
                of crashing

and intermingling—
        it's a strangeness of looping—
                of one action

cupped inside another action
        until the passing
                of topographic lines

become indecipherable—
        they're rendered invisible
                and undetected.

And now the couple bends
        to the beach
                to gather sea shells.

Suddenly she's colored beneath
        his topographic condition.
                I can't really *see* her,

because she's made herself
        undetectable inside
                his nomadic color.

And the man, too, is evaporating
             inside her stoppage
                        and her soft emergence:

he's being captured
             within her topography
                        of color;

her movement—toward him,
             around him—*gathers him,*
                        and, as I watch them,

I lose track of where her shoulders
             disappear within his,
                        and I can no longer

locate where his dominion
             and her isomorphic shape
                        dissolve, blend,

for they've become a strange
             looping *interweave*
                        within each another—

they're some form of unstable
             coloration that's now coalescing
                        and becoming a thing

entirely *else*—like a frequency hewing
             that doesn't ever cease.
                        I think they're like waves,

canceling each other's body line out
             at the crystallized glim point
                        of convergence—

and they're so gentle, yet so extreme.
             Isn't empathy truly like this:
                        that we blur

each other's margin line out
        at the point of glim convergence,
                only to mix and enter

into each other's sea shell
        of a limbic brain,
                like a pigmented

iridescence of wiggling fish?
        Don't our concerned thoughts
                and our loving gestures

with one another resemble curious fish
        just swimming through
                the strange looping

of our convergence zones?
        So active we seem to be—
                just to extend

and to be *co-mingled* with the other.
        Love's like a swimming channel:
                it's just a diverse,

divergent form of our greater roaming.
        And love must resemble
                a malleability slipstream:

it's like a quality of water: it splashes;
        it seeps; it resembles the horizon's
                blurred activity exchange:

it's an ever-changing and re-arranging
        blending contour, a looped tapestry,
                every hour.

And it's a seeding, for an imaginative realm
        that we *are* with one another:
                we leave seeds *in* one another,

and those seeds we leave—in history,
        in departure, in death, in dissolution,
                and in our love *for* one another—

are the strange loopings we live; and,
        in living them, we settle them to love,
                we complete them. Yes.

Look again at this contented couple I see:
        they're strolling farther away
                into the draw-out zone

of sunset going dark with the purple edging
        of another sundown;
                it's torqueing us orange-gold

in a catalytic, world-ending fire,
        all the while displaying to the whole beach
                precisely how to fade out

and yet, how never to fade out
        into the lonesome pulverization
                of these waves

landing straight on into the hydro-gloam
        of the shore.
                Maybe every color

that we are—whether holding hands together,
        or roaming apart—
                accords to us

a changing color tone value;
        a malleable notation
                that re-assembles itself constantly

like a train track where the switches
        are thrown
                like various sliders on a wire,

so that the two eventually merge as a third kind—
    all these inclinations, habits,
        and holographic hallucinations

that make up a total I-Thou—
    and frequently enough so,
        so that all this empathy,

all this engaged involvement,
    and all this energy exchange
        between us

and in everything else
    we give a heart-life to—
        never really ends.

The Water's Variation w/ Bird Feathers in it # 2

The water's sheen—blue lead,
    manganese, cobalt—
        coupled with

the rising vapor, so airy, part-frothed,
    part frayed and dense
        with chiaroscuro

and soft blending,
    and the blue of the sky
        and the surf tide—

mixing gold and jade splinters
    into a surface palette together—
        imparts a variation

so that the eyes,
    so puzzled at what to look at,
        dart left to right to find it,

this coloration
    so very like a prismatic butterfly
        as it erupts

across the jagged ridges
    of the chopped and chiseled waves
        that roll on

and recklessly drop
    into the harsh bedlam
        of a vagrant tumult

way out, in the soft outlier swells.
    We gather at the boat rails,
        mesmerized, looking out.

Isn't all beauty like this?
    One variation, blending
        within another—

so that all we witness
        must be seen by one eye
                and then

the other eye, complete?
        The repeated form or
                pattern to it—

variation—being the one clean motif
        we all must abide,
                or else one eye

loses forever the other eye's
        witness to what? To variety?
                The one eye—

so calculating for the obvious—
        while the other eye,
                a sleuth, goes roaming

for the one lost, immediate white object
        dissolving. Look at it: this lovely gull's feather
                we see floating

out there beyond us—
        like a bridal tulle or a veil
                into blue.

And the sea gulls, riding the wind,
        hypnotize themselves
                atop the blue foamed

roller coaster crest of the waves
        that rise and fall
                into sunset's funeral pyre

so that when we gaze out into it,
        this sundown,
                we no longer see

inside the golden kingdom of it
        just this one single feather—
                but *many, many feathers:*

whole groupings of bird feathers
        bouncing in the waves
                in a design variation

of gull and other bird feathers
        floating aimless and different,
                like a curated array.

And isn't variation just a seeing
        with multiple eyes?
                Aren't we already

prepped to see—
        with both our eyes
                working as witness—

all this diverse distinction
        gone scattershot,
                into splendor?

And isn't that
        how we all
                mature,

how we find original beauty,
        in a world
                made of pure awe?

Quartet for the End of Time

    —Louange a l'Immortalite de Jesus

I think it was the one violin's
        messa di voce

& that mastery of toned nuance
        that Messiaen

insisted the violinist play
        while he caressed the piano keys

low & solemnly
        so that the violin's feathery ascent

could lift the burdens of the body
        straight up

to Heaven
        just as the human nose, sniffing it,

could smell, in the acrid morning air,
        just how

the incinerated chambers of death
        might burn

the imprisoned body to bones & ashes
        & also,

so that the human eye could see
        how—amazingly—wealth & death

stand like emaciated men in juxtaposed
        happenstance,

& so he directed that the music
        be simple—

just a piano & a clarinet &
        a violin & cello—

& that it be accumulated,
	by adding the quartet together

so that the decrepit instruments,
	scrapped together

for a meager prison quartet,
	could play

for 400 inmates & armed guards
	at The Stalag VIII-A,

in Gorlitz, Germany, on a cold
	January day

in 1941.
	& also, in Eight Movements, so that

the pummeled ear drum could hear
	how we join

the calling up of the ascendant Spirit in that
	old game

of hide-&-seek when the immortality
	of Jesus

comes calling for us when we
	are tired & illuminated,

& we are done with this original ordeal
	of existence,

& how upward, in the ascent, we are
	made

divine in paradise—
	despite the brisk January wind,

& the ovens that would burn
> the innocent bodies, like wet doors.

& he directed that the violin solo
> evaporate in thin air

so that the winter birds too, could hear
> just what

all human vanishing sounds like
> when we

are without that heavy baggage—
> this impediment

of a human body so broken
> & bruised

by political torment. & so Messiaen
> directed

that the violinist's single solo flight,
> in its upward, climbing ascent,

be the answer to what's always
> speaking so silently

in the body, so that the
> hapless prison guards,

doing the will
> of a dead man

in an odd mustache
> & with knuckles crawling like black widow spiders

all over the maps of Europe
> & everywhere else,

could feel, in their inaudible
    cold bones,

what resurrection is,
    when it is the musical

expression
    of Thou Art One in God

rising upward, on the trembling
    strings of a violin

to its highest & softest
    if breathless harmonic,

& left there to linger in the ear
    as the last of our true senses to go.

& it is worn, too, like a prayer,
    all over the faces

of 400 prisoners of war
    in Gorlitz, Germany, in January, 1941,

taking absolutely nothing of themselves
    for the journey

but a thanksgiving
    within the immortality

of Jesus
    heard in the floating voice

of the Seventh Angel,
    intoning that

there shall be time no longer,
    for the quartet at the end of time

is nigh…
        & that we shall be finished

most resolute in God,
        & made right

in the greater moment of all this
        astounding music & grace.

Alive

Alive

Along the water's jagged crest, the waves
shatter into light.

They splash to the beach
like wheels & joints & jumbled hearts

humbled to gurgles; like a wet
surrendering made of pulleys,

shorn to foam & bubbles.
Some of the bubbles crush

like pearls. Some like iron,
or cream or stone. In one runnel,

the whole sky the bent shade
of a black trumpet mushroom.

In another trill rivulet a sling blade
of someone's body—maybe mine—

opalescent, obscure, appears,
shimmers there for a whole breath,

becomes an immense glistening,
like spilled cognac in the sun's

Byzantine haze.
I think some shadow of me is here,

waiting for the time that strikes in me
this endless love at first sight.

In another streak of shore water,
a suspended bird:

maybe it's a beach plover,
maybe a seagull or a stark tern

silhouetted in shadow
& just now the color of a baked tart;

it pauses there, shuddering,
just shivering the ice-melted shadow

of its winged self alive.
When I look at it

it's more striking
than the whole sky.

Springtime Invocation: White Baneberry

Wandering through these dense
      deciduous forests—
            now that the springtime

has massaged the winter cold
      and opened up the bronzed chalice
            of heat and sunlight

that's glazing to gold these field openings
      of reeds and swamp,
            of glade and forest—

I stop, bend low, find in my finger and thumb
      this wondrous white
            baneberry,

its ovular berries spotted with small,
      black doll's eyes
            wandering column-like

up a green stalk,
      and gazing straight up,
            at me.

Such hope it instils in me
      to discover it—
            this magic wand.

Such faith it brings
      back to me,
            when I least expected it,

so dense with introspection
      and with disquieted sorrow,
            and with last winter's

snow cave of memories
      not yet figured out,
            and heavy with these thoughts

of people I've lost
        to death's
                long sleep.

Such innocence! these
        one million eyes,
                gazing right back at me—

and looking right into me again—
        like I'm this sweet blindness,
                trying with light, to see.

The Mural Painter Graffiti Artist

—Dequindre Cut, Detroit

stands forthright, enraptured
by the light's mannerism

caught in varied coloration
on the edges of a broken

viaduct. &, consequently—
inspired within himself by

the miraculous & perilous
challenge of the afternoon's

sheen of light—he paints
the light in different strengths

& colors all across the
shattered cement, across

the formless monolith & across
its jagged fringed clefts & down

the sour-salt & corrosive lift
& largesse of it until

he discovers he's not painting
any form at all but rather,

the blaze itself, every loftless
variation of it, as if his own

eyes could barely get enough
of it, this light, this barely

containable, infidel mannerism
of it, these shafts of light

so ambient & so transcendent,
fading & exploding near.

His heart's of equal tension—
lost between objective clarity

& the cognitive dissonance
of the blaze's surrendering

into heat
& that thirsty hot sheen

that the the day's escape
into yellow-orange

is made of. & of the image:
the clown's face, emerging

in the center, wiggles & it gleams.
He dabs it, puts pigment into it—

this sole refugee of the last light's
softened drum & silent hue;

& he rounds the face in violet, in
greens & blues, in scatter light,

this bull's-eye laughing face
suddenly radiant & hilarious;

& he grooves a jagged grin
inside it so as to enliven it—this

clown's inner emotional mood
of hysterical light—so that

when we stumble onto it,
here on our Saturday stroll—

the haggard landscape of the
city's irregular boxed buildings

fixed & solid behind us—
the clown seems to guffaw

right back into the rays
of the sunset's simple, if rabid

explosion of glow.
& the painter's signature,

just a tic-tac-toe of
Xs & Os in a slant

of zig-zag lines,
slips right out

of the mural
like name & art, at play.

James Brown, Performing at the Apollo, 1962

splits and limps and stumbles
        down to his knees on the stage,
                caped, sweat-drenched

like a drugged demiurge—
        something part ogre,
                part demon-in-the-making—

so that when the side-kick
        rushes out to assist him,
                pull him up from his bent knees

to the church altar
        of the Apollo Theater Stage,
                the kids sitting front row

are splashed by the sweat
        lifting dog-shook
                from his horse-shaped

muscled neck.
        And now he grips the mic
                and starts into please, please, please,

so that for generations
        the kids will know
                for the rest of their lives

how far a preacher goes
        with torment
                and hard-packed lust,

engaging
        in heart-pleading
                spectacle—

which is a combination of Harlem shuffle
        and Pentecostal Oratory
                mixed into a man's world,

which is why the kids see the perspiration
        of ecstatic impulse
                forever streaked

across the singer's panicked,
        heat-stroked
                neck and forehead.

And as they push forward to study him—
        as he burns the good foot
                from his dance step—

they won't ever forget
        how a man kicks out the sin
                from his groin and hip

in a rabble-rousing preacher's march
        of drop-bow-and-step
                across a wooden stage.

And now he wiggles left to right,
        and he pranks
                the camel walk

into a forward traveling slide
        and then, for kicks,
                he rolls the squiggly

mashed potato
        into the funky chicken
                and down

to the boogaloo to split—
        which is part shake-shake
                sugaree,

part soul-funk affliction,
        part epileptic fit,
                part hound dog

shriek-and-shrill
        kneed into a heart-
                pleading-prayer

drenched in trill:
        which is how a man,
                his brain on holy fire,

joins with lust and prayer—
        to sex machine
               it in.

The Angel of the Wonderful

The young woman at the counter, masked
in a bandana because of the pandemic,

smiled a floral smile with her eyes at me.
I'd placed a dozen pink roses before her.

She picked stealthily at the faded petals,
one by one, removing those dull, wrinkled

petals already withered by long days
in the cool storage fridge and I, because I

couldn't help my loneliness, offered up
to her a comment that, on a brand new day,

I might see the smile behind her scarf
breaking into a delirium of cardinals catching flame.

And she, not missing a point, said, you too,
and when I complimented her quick

paced fingers, clipping the dull petals
from each worshiped rose, she said briskly

to me, "No unhappy roses sold here:
Only happy roses for the ones we love."

And something of the air, an audience,
lighted, and when I left her—my arms

full of pink roses right there in love's body—
I was the one. I was infinite. Oh Yes.

And on that warm morning when we
studied the small gray sparrows mating

in the clematis—right there in a hulk-
pod formed like an oval in the tangle—

my wife whispered, "they're mating in there,"
and the angel of the wonderful said,

real presence always holds the eternal
in it. And I said, loving something is a

cleansing of it, and the angel, empty
of God because it was here in my yard

and borrowing a matter of days in form,
said to me, yes, the light of all manna

falls like traced God from upper space, it hangs—
it hangs like flora in the open air

and that is the yearning we all feel—
feeling it—and those not yet dulled

or obliterated by a self consumed by what's
already been stolen from it,

touch it, and they enjoy holding onto it,
this manna—and they allow their yearning to test

the test of time until they, too, are
won over by the ceremony of the wonderful;

and what was a dull patina on them brightens,
in this, the wonderful, like fresh-grown roses.

And the two small glorified sparrows
hovered in the hovel; and the one,

behind the other, tagged her, he tagged her
oh so gently, and he entered her

like a feathered fullness voiding himself
of unstrained light while the other,

the female, like a small oven, a dust rose,
moved backward, inward, all light.

What I Love About the Evening's Sunset (A Postcard)

What I love about the evening's sunset, falling like a drunken gypsy lover into the velvet blue of his rising lover—the embracing ocean—swelled so

very wide and flush with the afterglow of dusk's baked lasagna, is the sleek way that his skin peels into yellow and then shimmers into stripes of clam-

colored pink and boiled lobster and then purple chalk, and, afterwards, all the rest of him descends into streaks of aqua-marine and enlarged shades

of midnight blue until the ocean's stagger and its lurch wraps her wide sea's arms around him. Who knew such color could be held inside the sunlight,

surrendering itself to the finality of a day? Who knew a man could embrace something so much greater? So much bigger than himself and all his small

ideas—so grandiose—and so fat with the day's soft absence; its last wheat beer glow. All my life I have been waiting for the slip and fall into an

expansive glow. For the broken hour glass of *oh hell yes*—I'm falling into your arms forever: the whole figure eight shape of me, my elbow tips

and my arms, my hips, my heavy bones and my head tossed wide, like a muskmelon Faberge egg so excited and yolked with passion and just nose-

diving and somersaulting, face-first, into the languid sprawl and embrace of you—sweet indigo lover—corralling all of me into your violet air, into

your ocean's lupine glow. See all this: what's happening to me! Me, a man, dissolving into the sunset's roasted-pepper show. My sunny disposition,

melting, igniting, streaming the rest of my self behind! My staunch heat, burnt, surrendered, my punch-drunk half-light and my topsy-turvy old gold

sorcery, all of it, gone slip-sliding—drunken, in a jolly reverie—into the wet soufflé of your ocean's arms, into the lush vibrant curves of your body, uprising. Who knew I was ready for a fall so deep? To collapse—the ready-willing all of me, my head thrown back, alert, laughing, downward, sinking

into the rollicking wet tumult of you, my ocean lover, my wide wide open-hearted sea.

That Perfume Fragrance You Smelled in Grasse

1.

Jasmine, those fragrant, star-shaped flowers, when plucked
from the open-throated collar of the green plant at dawn,

there in the plush fields of Grasse by young girls gathering them
in wicker baskets, make a small *squeak*—
    as if their red-hearted centers were complaining—

a small wince of pain at the center of every claiming of beauty.

2.

    And the *Provence rose*—

like a young bride excited by the pink flushing of her cheeks
    at her wedding nuptials in May,

is called by the men who gather her to them by a special lover's
    name they hold for her: *rose de mai*.

And the workers, with their eager hands, become delirious
    within the roses' shoulder-high wedding dresses—

doomed there to inhale forever into their open nostrils
the musky, ethereal scent of rosewater essence amidst the moist

showcase of petals, wet with morning's delicate dew—
    as if the roses had pink bodices, tipped

    in the dawn's light.

3.

And when the purple-blue sprawl of lavender gardens ripple
and rinse a floral pine essence across the hot Provence pavement,

the men on tractors descending down from the mountain roads,
    stop—
enticed to inhale the perfume of her: *lavandula angustifolia,*

this potpourri in a sachet, meaning one who washes clean the sweat
of labor from a man's licorice-tanned skin.

Meaning that all attraction
        is aroma. Is the elixir of the nose in all of us, enlivened.
And meaning too, that the aromas of the world, enter our soul.

                4.

It doesn't have to be this intense—
        you think to yourself as you write this poem
about the power of perfume and fragrance—

even the words for it excite:

        bee honey in a pot-belly,
        white extract of vanilla,

powder-scented mimosa flowers in a farmer's straw hat,

purple plumes of iris sprouting erect in a porcelain vase
on the end table of a motel by the turn of the sea;

orange blossoms from Tunisia spread across a bed sheet
        long after a hike on the shore,

or, say, round balls of green mandarins tossed into a bucket from Sicily
where you once walked with her, the both of you reading
        that book on perfume;

or the smoky, orange crystal limelight of ginger bits
gathered into a glass bowl,

        your fingers digging deep for the sharp,
burning tang of the sting on your tongue
        before you embraced her, inside the floral drapery

of the jacquard lace curtains at that Victorian Hotel
somewhere in the middle of Michigan,

where the two of you stayed on the 1st anniversary
of your marriage; the florid taste of fragrance

like some mysterious line of desire to be crossed
between lovers making haste to arrive;—

5.

it doesn't have to be this intense, but it is: these flower fragments
smell like they've been ripped and culled from something earthen
    and thrilling, something *woman*—

something reckless and magic: as if *intensity itself* had a quality
    of perfume to it: some physical, thermal

extracted formula of odor. It doesn't have to be this intense,
    but it is:

perfume of multiplied color, perfume of hands stirring flung petals
    together;

floral odors mixed, exhausted like satisfied lovers bound together
in mid-afternoon play, their sweat and fragrance

passing through a chimney where a lone perfumer in Grasse
    does his life's work;—

    and look at this beauty:

perfume of jasmine rising in an ethereal mist to the high ceiling
    of a laboratory by the flick of his gloved hand,

released free to the open expansive air;—

    and look at this beauty:

vats of stunned flower heads and tables of astonished petals
stirred to arousal and summation

                and then cooled in big jugs and laid out flat
on a square glass frame in a thick goop of jellied, odorless fat
until the fat is saturated by the exhausted extraction of aroma,
        the flower's fragrant essence:—

and then it is slipped, like silk, into a bottle of *Eau de Cologne*.
The one elegant bottle of it we purchased, in Grasse, France.

6.

    It doesn't have to be this intense, but it is:

wilted petals—nearly a ton of them—
fading thereafter into silent, distilled nothingness,

so that they then blossom into an enfleurage pomade
        of colorless, evaporated fat and flavor,

and then, into a miracle of theft and alchemy, this creation of cologne
        and perfume from one single flower—

this extraction and composition of aroma, together.

    It doesn't have to be this intense, but it is:

this glass bottle of perfume, standing here before you.

7.

It makes you envision your wife's outstretched body,
lying in summation in a bed of exquisite aroma:

the body of a woman you love, wearing her night's fragrance.

It doesn't have to be this intense you say aloud again
        to yourself: but it is: it is.

Valentine w/ A Sentence in it

Some valentines have sentences in them first.
That's why everything I loved, in one moment,

changed when you interrupted me.
All love is an interruption of that

madness that makes us believe what we write.
Truth is, we are vocabularies interrupted

by other vocabularies and when you
interrupted my long sentence, like I was

writing it alone in a classroom, on
a chalk board for what seemed like a hundred

years, I lifted the eraser in my right
hand and I started erasing my own

sentence because what you had to say,
in your sentence, was much more

interesting. And the trick was that, as I
erased my sentence with my right hand,

I tried not to remember it because love is
a kind of non-remembering of the self,

and—because the self is dense, like a treatise,
or a paragraph, or filibuster monologue—

it's best to forget it—the self—and place
a firmer faith in the spontaneous,

and love is quicker, and it walks in a lightness
of ease like a quickly sketched sentence

writ eternal and writ memorable,
and the light fell on the cherry tree

where the other woman was reading
her book, and the farmer, plowing his field

on a tractor, did what anyone would do
when they are interrupted: he stopped

for a moment, cupped a hand over
his brow, and so did the woman,

and they watched us from a distance
with eyes, large as awe-struck sunflowers

as you interrupted me with sentences
so much more interesting than my own,

and I responded to you by erasing
more of me and writing my response back,

and they stood there silently together
watching us with wide open eyes

writing and re-writing our sentence
on the blackboard and out the door

and across the sidewalks and into
the world of corn there where nobody

could stop us, and so they just looked
at us like the world was ending; and

they followed us with ravenous eyes
because we're all interested in sentences,

and we're all vocabularies just wanting
to be interrupted by another vocabulary,

and the world changed from one page, or
a blackboard, or a cornfield, and into

a shifting grid of words and shapes writ
on a page without edit or ending;

and writ in a style of cursive where one
line follows the next line in a kind

of immeasurable hide and seek and chase
and follow, from one edge over another

like two water striders streaking quickly
over the expanse of an empty white page

so that the chase, and return, could find
that next page and the page after that—

and go on and on like that, just like a
wondrous line that never really ends—

and love is a sentence you write or scribble
until it is unnecessary to write it any

longer and, when it is no longer, the
valentine you take is the ♥ of your life.

The Light at the Edge of the Dining Room Table

has my whole life in it; even when I tried to become a big fish

or a bird or a cat or a cicada trying to sing one sensational song.
Every life is a pastoral, just an ode to the light at the edge

of the dining room table where we eat, where we break bread,
where we speak to one another about what love is, or what hurts us,

or what make us cry like a fountain made of stars falling out of eyes.
To say yes to the world means one more life counts for the earth's

simple bargain with us. To hold a bird in one's hand is to feel what a star is,
when it is shining with all its might. To kiss is to play dice with a mystery.

To pet the cat, my little cat named Olive, makes me smile like a galaxy,
because the color of the night sky is what breathes life into all our days

and she's not trying to prove anything to a year's calendar except
that it matters to nap in the light at the edge of the dining room table.

The light at the edge of the dining room table doesn't seem to care a wit
about all my memories. All it does is act like I'm there, just keeping

count of what energy is made of when it slants direct across wood,
and one is left with excitement, or what Spirit is without my two cents.

God created words because we couldn't describe him. This is what a hiker
told me in the Blue Ridge Mountains. We were hiking together.

We were up in the rhododendron gardens; he was divorcing his wife
or rather, she was leaving him for another person; we drank beer

and we pretended we understood what dying and love was made of,
and he told me, God created all these words so that we could describe

what the light at the edge of a table feels like when we are lost in it.
He was drinking, and when the fire petered out he blubbered like love

does when it drains into that unsteady brook of memory and forgetting. It slaughters something deep in us, he said to me. Yes it does.

It's forged in light, and it makes a divine value pass from what is skin into what, at once, is but a nameless introduction to something vaster.

I told him nothing is wrong except that we use words to describe what the world is trying to say to us by how it won't ever answer us.

The light at the edge of the dining room table is Spiritual consent, saying Come unto me; the world is what cries us awake when we give love to it.

Wilderness State Park Epistle

"I am freed from the burdens of the sea when the waters come towards me"
—Vallejo

Because the winterberry's knuckles have glowing red berries on them,
& also small corsages of green leaves pinned like wings to fingers,

& the gnarled shore oaks shiver like half-dressed skeletons-in-waiting
beneath a lonesome wind where young couples—warm from this

afternoon's beach party—snuggle together around logs cut for a fire
& they practice being married &, also, because the beach is windswept

& unruly & full of abandoned nights, & because it howls & it sours
like a sudden country music song gone ill, gone astray with bad content,

I have to write this epistle to you because a love letter depends on it.
"Everything is an imitation of Christ," said Thomas a Kempis, that

Augustinian monk writing in his solitude & trying to work his way
to grace; &, maybe, what he meant, is that all love is a nuptial with time,

& our knuckles have red berries on them &, because of it, something
of us is sacrificed on an up-scraped hill, &, to be made a priest involves

a silence & also a waiting, & a lying still under the first autumn-mad stars
that smoke brightly in the sky like snow lilies, trying to spark a beach fire.

———

I used to believe prayer was desire, made holy. That our fingers, steepled,
could make another church. But because the winterberry's knuckles have

red berries on them &, because they bleed, & the green leaves, shivering
in the wind, are corsages on bound fingers reaching up into the unknown

universe to find a nuptial & a tribulation that is—somehow, no matter
how we speak to it anyway—*sweet*—& because we are the first suffering

that releases its God-resistance—all this hunger that does not eat—
I have to write this epistle to you…the *you* who eludes me…because

you are a white-laced window, shuddering in a silent hotel over a lake,
& I am a glowing fleck of fire; I'm swirling prayers, in ash-blown smoke.

———

We are a successive ordeal of incarnations, I think. & we are here to follow
an inward solitude that tells us we are no one & that we're anonymous

before a grace that will not tell us what to see or do. Tell me it isn't true?
We are just pages being written on. Providences made of sweetness, loss.

Our natures trampled upon by shifting eddies of wanderlust stars, in
a smoked sky that doesn't even acknowledge us, nor offer to us a living

holy name unless we reach into it, our hands cupped & empty & hungry
for a glowing fleck of light & for a sacred name we'd own. Its light, freeing

us like a saint. & we're led to faith by a hope in crops & by prayers to a sun
& a moon that confess to us—each day—their cold liturgies like lost

pronouncements in another language &, also, by a cattle herd of
constellations we give Greek names to—for company—just because we are

faithful—anyway & anyhow—& we're loyal—always—to that cold
namelessness that holds a greater claim to that mysterious hotel above us.

———

& the young couples, lighting camp fires here in Wilderness State Park &
sipping their beers & pretending to be married under the first desolate stars,

are resurrections into that ongoing heavenly trance. & they are living free
& they're holy. & they will be subsumed to the sun & the moon & to a Great

Lakes freighter that reflects the night sky in it as it lumbers all the cold way
to St. Lawrence. The end of us follows a full consent into the unknown, I

can tell you that. & then, we are priests & lovers to a solitary call that
divines us. & it is unbearable. & it is holy. & it is on the other side of a

white-laced window floating above the lake, & I want it. It's been arranged
this way & I am its tenant. This is what the red winterberries on my knuckles

say to me when I look down at them & I spread the green corsages of leaves
open to find my vineyard fingers. & to You, I say—oh invincible perimeter

of wilderness night sky without a name—I am awakened in you—always—
& I am engraved in you & I am staring into that white-laced window over

the lake. & I am at home in all that smoke, & I'm praying to it—yes—
to that other life. & I'm glowing like a fleck of fire, praying to a God

hid in smoke; & I am at home in all that smoke; & I am a doomed hotel
with its rooftop & its walls lit up on fire. & I believe in it, oh yes.

All the World, A Stage

At the intimate moment of fire,
        they held hands
                outside the barn,

watched the fire
        consuming the whole building,
                popping it like confetti stars.

They saw the black apple trees
        catching flame,
                saw the open yard

where the horses run
        igniting up,
                the hay wagon, combusting,

the water trough filling up
        with watery ash,
                with flames-of-mourning,

and they saw the roadside
        bursting into
                corn-colored cashew;

and they watched
        the old hickory tree exploding,
                the rope swing on it

rocking back
        and forth,
                ghosted in feral smoke,

and they saw
        the clouds above them
                expanding with lungs

of purple;
        and, game birds—
                grouse, lark,

wild duck, pheasant—
        suddenly escaping
                into herald and haze,

the sky above them
        now garbanzo bean,
                now garlic,

now slices of fibrous rhubarb,
        collard greens, heat—
                as if all the horizon

could be exhumed, at dusk;
        and they saw the church steeple
                in the blue distance

piercing the ganache
        of skylight
                like a sewing needle,

and they watched the first stars
        rising distant
                like salt and pepper,

the new moon, hanging heavily
        like someone's
                soda cracker.

She held a box saw
        in her hand. He opened up
                an accordion,

and, slowly,
        he pumped it
                into sound

while the farmhouse,
        beyond them,
                glowed

like a tabernacle
        of the day's last
                fire:

something filled with
        hope and awe
                and glory:

and they saw the sun,
        setting behind it,
                all the world, a stage.

About the Author

Ken Meisel is a poet and psychotherapist from the Detroit area. He is a 2012 Kresge Arts Literary Fellow, Pushcart Prize nominee, Swan Duckling chapbook contest winner, winner of the Liakoura Prize and the author of eight poetry collections: **Our Common Souls: New & Selected Poems of Detroit** (Blue Horse Press: 2020) **Mortal Lullabies** (FutureCycle Press: 2018), **The Drunken Sweetheart at My Door** (FutureCycle Press: 2015), **Scrap Metal Mantra Poems** (Main Street Rag: 2013), **Beautiful Rust** (Bottom Dog Press: 2009), **Just Listening** (Pure Heart Press: 2007), **Before Exiting** (Pure Heart Press: 2006) and **Sometimes the Wind** (March Street Press: 2002). His work is in over 100 national magazines including *Cream City Review, Rattle, Dressing Room Poetry Journal, Midwestern Gothic, Concho River Review, San Pedro River Review, Boxcar Review, Origins Journal, The Bookends Review, Muddy River Poetry Review, Pirene's Fountain, Lake Effect, Soundings East, Gravel Magazine,* and *Lullwater.*

He was the featured poet interview in *Rattle* Magazine's September, 2017 "Rust Belt Issue" and the featured poet in the movie, *Detroit: Tough Luck Stories* (2019).

www.ingramcontent.com/pod-product-compliance
Lightning Source LLC
Chambersburg PA
CBHW032004080426
42735CB00007B/506